Germany

Sue Townsend

Heinemann
Library
Chicago, Illinois

© 2002 Reed Educational & Professional Publishing
Published by Heinemann Library,
an imprint of Reed Educational & Professional Publishing,
Chicago, Illinois

Customer Service 888-454-2279

Visit our website at www.heinemannlibrary.com

Designed by Tinstar Design
Illustrations by Nicholas Beresford-Davies
Originated by Dot Gradations
Printed by Wing King Tong in Hong Kong

06 05 04 03 02
10 9 8 7 6 5 4 3 2 1

Library of Congress Cataloging-in-Publication Data
Townsend, Sue, 1963-
   Germany / Sue Townsend.
     p. cm. -- (A world of recipes)
   Includes bibliographical references and index.
   Summary: A collection of recipes from Germany, plus cultural and
nutritional information.
   ISBN 1-58810-610-1
   1. Cookery, German--Juvenile literature. [1. Cookery, German.]   I.
Title. II. Series
  TX721 .T68 2002
  641.5943--dc21
                              2001004807

Acknowledgments
The Publishers would like to thank the following for permission to reproduce photographs:
p. 5 Corbis; all other photographs Gareth Boden.

Cover photographs reproduced with permission of Gareth Boden.

Every effort has been made to contact copyright holders of any material reproduced in this book. Any omissions will be rectified in subsequent printings if notice is given to the publisher.

Some words are shown in bold, **like this.** You can find out what they mean by looking in the glossary.

Contents

German Food

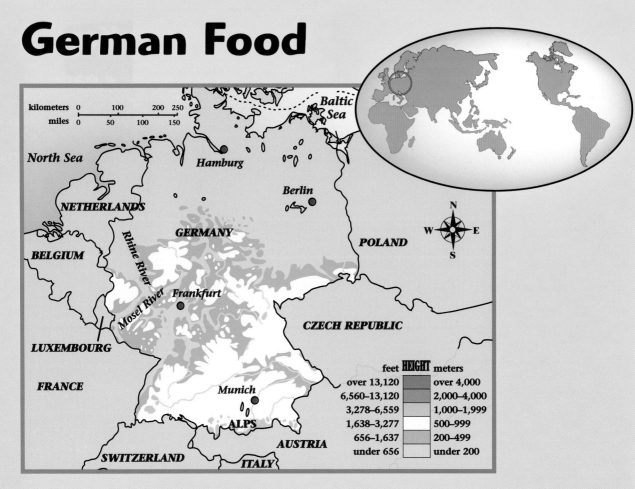

Germany is in the middle of Europe. The land is very varied, with sandy beaches in the north and the snowy peaks of the Alps mountains to the south.

Around the country

The northern and eastern areas of Germany are low and flat. It can be cold and wet here, so people like to eat warming foods, such as soups and roasted meats. Pickled meats and herring are also popular. People in this region like to add lemon juice or vinegar to their food for a sour taste.

The middle of Germany has many forests and river valleys. Hams made from wild pigs are specialties here, as well as Bratwurst sausages, sauerkraut (cabbage **fermented** with salt), and potato dumplings. Vineyards and orchards produce grapes, apples, and pears. Rye, a grain used for making bread, is also grown here.

▶ *Many German towns have open-air markets that sell a wide variety of fresh foods.*

In the south it is more hilly. Cows graze here, and grapevines grow along the Mosel and Rhine river valleys. Farmers here also grow wheat for making bread.

In the past

For hundreds of years, Germany was made up of small kingdoms ruled by princes who enjoyed hunting and roasting the meat they caught on open fires. Feasts then often lasted as long as eight hours. Today, Germany, like the United States, is made up of many states (called *Länder*). Each state is different, so Germany has many styles of cooking and special regional dishes.

German meals

Germans enjoy simple, hearty meals. Breakfast (*frühstück*) consists of a choice of breads, jam, and cold meats. Cheeses, boiled eggs, yogurt, fruit juice, and small pastries may also be served, especially on the weekend. Lunch (*mittagessen*) is usually the main meal of the day and often includes dumplings, noodles, or potatoes with meat. Dessert might be gelatin with fruit, or a slice of cake (*gâteau*).

The evening meal (*abendessen*) may consist of a cold meal of open-face sandwiches or a cold meat platter with gherkins (small pickles), radishes, and tomatoes. Germans also enjoy a number of festivals during the year in which food, wine, and beer play an important part.

Ingredients

beets

cabbage

bread

sausage

sauerkraut

radishes

cold meats

gherkins

cheese

apples

mushrooms

morello
cherries

pears

sausage

Bread
German bread is often made with rye flour, which has a rich, nutty taste. German bakeries offer a wide range of bread and rolls. Outside Germany you can buy German breads from larger supermarkets.

Dill
Dill is a common herb in German food. Dill seeds often flavor pickles. They taste a little bit like black licorice.

Fruit
Apples and pears are plentiful in Germany and are often made into juice. Apple, pear, and other types of fruit juices are favorite German drinks.

Ham
German hams are cured, which means they are soaked in very salty water. They are also smoked by hanging them over a smoky fire for a long time. Burning different woods in the fire gives the hams different flavors.

Morello cherries

Morello cherries have a slightly sour taste. You can find them in the supermarket in jars or cans in a sugar syrup.

Pickles

Any vegetable or fruit that is preserved in vinegar is called a pickle. Gherkins are small pickled cucumbers. They are sold in jars and flavored with dill and other spices. Pickled beets are a favorite in Germany, too.

Sauerkraut

Sauerkraut is white cabbage that has been layered with salt and allowed to **ferment**. It has a sharp, tangy taste. You can buy it in large jars in supermarkets. Germans eat it with hot or cold meats and sausage.

Sausage

Sausage is very popular in Germany, and there are many kinds to choose from. Bratwurst is pork or veal sausage that needs to be fried or grilled. Schinkenwurst is ham sausage. Bierwurst is a pork and beef sausage that is cut into thick slices and grilled. You should be able to find some of these types of sausage at your local supermarket.

Cheese

The most popular cheese in Germany is called Speisequark, or quark. It is ideal as a dip, spread onto bread, or baked in a cheesecake (see page 36). You can find it in most larger supermarkets. Another favorite cheese is Tilsut, a creamy yellow cheese with little holes in it. People in Germany often serve a selection of cheeses with a cold meat platter as a meal with bread and pickles.

Before You Begin

Kitchen rules

There are a few basic rules you should always follow when you cook:

- Ask an adult if you can use the kitchen.

 • Some cooking processes, especially those involving hot water or oil, can be dangerous. When you see this sign, take extra care or ask an adult to help.
- Wash your hands before you start.
- Wear an apron to protect your clothes. Tie back long hair.
- Be very careful when using sharp knives.
- Never leave pan handles sticking out—it could be dangerous if you bump into them.
- Always wear oven mitts when lifting things in and out of the oven.
- Wash fruits and vegetables before using them.

How long will it take?

Some of the recipes in this book are quick and easy, and some are more complicated and take longer. The strip across the top of the right-hand page of each recipe tells you how long it will take to cook each dish from start to finish. It also shows how difficult each dish is to make:

* (easy), ** (medium), or *** (difficult).

Quantities and measurements

You can see how many people each recipe will serve at the top of each right-hand page, too. Most of the recipes in this book make enough to feed two or four people. You can multiply or divide the quantities if you want to cook for more or fewer people.

Ingredients for recipes can be measured in two ways. Imperial measurements use cups and ounces. Metric measurements use grams and milliliters. In these recipes you will see the following abbreviations:

tbsp = tablespoon   oz = ounce
tsp = teaspoon   lb = pound
ml = milliliter   cm = centimeter
g = gram   mm = millimeter

Utensils

To cook the recipes in this book, you will need these utensils, as well as kitchen essentials such as spoons, plates, and bowls:

- cutting board
- food processor or blender
- nonstick frying pan
- ovenproof casserole dish
- rolling pin
- electric mixer
- sieve
- small and large saucepans with lids
- measuring spoons
- measuring cups
- sharp knife
- baking sheets
- round cake tins
- colander
- icing **piping** kit
- parchment paper
- bread pan
- grater
- **Dutch oven**
- ladle

 Whenever you see this symbol, be very careful.

Pancake Soup

Winter can be very cold in Germany so people eat a lot of warming soups. This soup is made more filling by adding slices of pancake to it. Make the pancakes first, and add them to the soup just before serving.

What you need

½ cup (60 g) flour
1 egg
½ cup (125 ml) milk
2 tsp vegetable oil
2 beef, chicken, or vegetable stock cubes
2 tbsp fresh **chopped** chives or parsley, to **garnish**

What you do

1 Put the flour into a bowl.

2 Lightly **beat** the egg and milk together.

3 Add half the egg and milk mixture to the flour and stir.

4 Gradually beat in the rest of the milk and egg to make a pancake batter.

5 Put some of the oil into a nonstick frying pan. Heat it on low heat. Tilt the pan to spread the oil around. Add 1 to 2 tablespoons of pancake batter and tilt the pan so that the batter spreads out thinly.

6 Cook the pancake for two to three minutes until it starts to become firm and is golden brown underneath. Turn the pancake using a spatula and cook it until both sides are lightly browned. Slide it onto a plate. Follow steps 5 and 6 until all the pancake batter is used.

7 Roll up all pancakes and cut them into very thin strips.

8 Put 3 ½ cups (825 ml) of water into a saucepan. Crumble in the stock cubes and heat until **simmering**. Add the pancake strips and heat for 1 minute.

9 Ladle into soup bowls. Scatter chives or parsley over each bowl and serve hot.

Rye Bread

Rye flour makes dark bread with a strong flavor. Rye bread is a common type of bread in Germany. It's very firm, so it is a popular choice for making open-face sandwiches with meats and cheeses.

What you need

3 cups (350 g) rye flour
3 cups (350 g)
   whole wheat flour
½ tsp salt
1 ¼-oz (7-g) packet
   active dry yeast
3 tbsp vegetable oil
3 tbsp honey
¾ cup (175 ml)
   lukewarm water
½ cup (110 ml)
   lukewarm milk

What you do

1 Put the flour, salt, and yeast into a bowl or food processor. Add the oil, honey, water, and milk to make a soft but not sticky dough. (If using a food processor, slowly add the liquid through the funnel until the dough forms a ball.)

2 **Knead** the dough ten minutes by hand or three minutes with a food processor (see page 13).

3 Put the dough into a bowl. Rub a little oil over a piece of plastic wrap. **Cover** the bowl with the plastic wrap (oil side down) and leave it in a warm place to rise for about one hour or until the dough has doubled in size.

4 Knead the dough again, five minutes by hand or two to three minutes in a food processor.

5 Form the dough into a brick shape and put it into a large loaf pan. Press the dough into the corners. Cover with oiled plastic wrap and leave in a warm place for 40 minutes to rise again.

6 Preheat the oven to 425°F (210°C).

7 **Bake** the loaf for 25 to 30 minutes, or until the bread sounds hollow when you tap it.

8 Allow the loaf to cool in the pan for ten minutes, then take it out of the pan and place it on a wire rack to cool before **slicing** and serving.

KNEADING DOUGH

To knead dough by hand, put the dough on a floured surface and stretch it toward you with one hand. Then fold the dough in half and press down on it with your palm. Turn it a little, pull it toward you, and fold it again. Keep repeating this until the dough becomes stretchy.

USEFUL YEAST

Yeast is a living thing. If it is made warm and given food, it will grow and produce bubbles. These bubbles of air are what make foods like bread rise. High temperatures kill the yeast, so any liquid added to dough with yeast in it should only be warm, not hot.

Cold Meat Platter

Platters of deli meats are very popular in Germany. People often serve them for the evening meal along with pickles, or as part of a special breakfast.

What you need

4 eggs
8 oz (230 g) deli meats such as bierwurst, salami, and Westphalian ham
8 slices of German bread or rolls, or some of each
8 gherkins

What you do

1 Put the eggs into a saucepan. **Cover** them with water, bring to a **boil**, and **simmer** for ten minutes.

2 Meanwhile, arrange the meats on a large plate. Start with the larger slices, then add the smaller slices, rolling or folding some of them so they look interesting.

3 Lift the eggs out of the pan with a spoon. Place them in a bowl of cold water, refilling it with fresh cold water as they cool.

4 When the eggs have cooled, **peel** off the shells. Cut the eggs into halves, quarters, or slices. Arrange them around the meats.

5 **Slice** each gherkin lengthwise three times without cutting all the way to the end. Spread the slices out into a fan.

6 Arrange the gherkins on the meat platter. Serve with a selection of German breads, butter, and extra gherkins.

GERMAN MEATS

There are over 80 types of meat, sausage, and ham in Germany. Sausages range from spicy to mild in flavor, and from smooth to coarse in texture. Choose a variety of meats to make an interesting meat platter.

GERMAN BREADS

There are over 200 different varieties of German bread. Keep an eye out for Vollkornbrot (full-grain rye bread), which goes well with cheese and ham. Landbrot is Germany's everyday bread and is made with rye and wheat flours. Another favorite, pumpernickel, is a strongly flavored dark rye bread.

Herring in Sour Cream

A herring is a small fish. Germans eat herring in a variety of ways—smoked, pickled, sprinkled with a flavored oil, or added to salads. This recipe is for a German favorite, herring in an onion and sour cream **marinade**.

What you need

4 pickled herring
2 tbsp lemon juice
⅔ cup (150 ml) sour cream
¼ cup (60 ml) plain yogurt
1 onion
1 apple
1 tsp fresh dill, **chopped**
sprigs of dill to **garnish**

What you do

1 Put a colander over a bowl. Place the herring in the colander and allow them to **drain**.

2 Mix together the lemon juice, sour cream, and yogurt.

3 **Peel** the onion and **slice** it into thin rings.

4 Cut the apple into quarters and cut out the core. Cut three of the pieces into small cubes.

5 Stir the onion, apple, and chopped dill into the sour cream mixture. Gently toss the herring in the mixture to coat them.

6 Put the herring on a serving dish and spoon the sauce around them. Slice the remaining piece of apple and use it and the sprigs of dill to garnish the dish.

SOUR CREAM

Sour cream that you buy in the supermarket has been made by adding a special ingredient to cream that makes it turn sour. You should not use cream that has simply gone bad in place of sour cream. You can, however, make your own sour cream at home. To make your own, add 1 teaspoon lemon juice to ⅔ cup (150 ml) cream and allow the cream to thicken for 30 minutes.

Pork and Apple Casserole

Meat and fruit are often served together in Germany. This hearty dish from northern Germany is ideal for a winter day. The long, slow method of cooking makes the pork very tender. The apple thickens the stock to make a tangy sauce.

What you need

2 onions
1 tbsp vegetable oil
4 thick pork chops
1 vegetable stock cube
½ tsp dried thyme
½ tsp dried oregano
½ tsp dried sage
½ tsp dried parsley
1 tsp caraway seeds
20 to 25 small
   button mushrooms
1 large apple

What you do

1 Preheat the oven to 350°F (180°C).

2 Peel the onions and **slice** them thinly.

3 Heat the oil over high heat in a large **Dutch oven**. **Fry** the onions for two minutes.

4 Add the pork chops and cook for three minutes on one side, or until browned. Turn them over and brown the other side.

5 Crumble the stock cube in 2 ½ cups (600 ml) hot water and stir until it dissolves. Add the dried herbs, caraway seeds, and stock to the Dutch oven. Bring to a **boil** and **cover**.

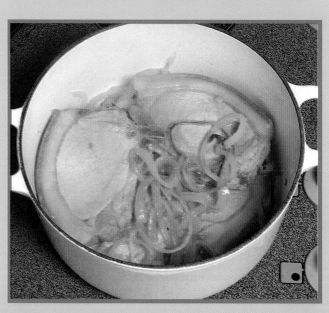

6 Wearing oven mitts, carefully put the casserole into the oven to cook.

7 After 1 ½ hours of cooking time, clean the mushrooms. Peel the apple and remove the core. **Chop** the apple.

8 Add the mushrooms and apple to the casserole. Make sure they are covered with liquid. Add extra hot water if necessary.

9 Cover and cook for 25 more minutes, or until the apple is very soft and the mushrooms are tender.

10 Serve hot with boiled potatoes or potato dumplings (page 28).

Pork and Beef Rissoles

The American hamburger has its beginnings in Germany, in the town of Hamburg. These rissoles are a common dish in Germany and are similar to what we call hamburgers. Both ground beef and pork are used to give them a rich flavor.

What you need

4 oz (115 g) ground pork
4 oz (115 g) ground beef
1 thick slice stale bread
1 small onion
1 egg
1 tbsp vegetable oil
1 tomato

What you do

1 Mix the pork and beef together with a fork.

2 Cut the bread into quarters. Put into a blender or food processor and process to make bread crumbs.

3 **Peel** the onion. **Slice** off a few rings and set them aside. Finely **chop** the rest.

4 Lightly **beat** the egg. Mix together the meat, bread, onion, egg, and a little salt and pepper.

5 Using half of the meat mixture, form it into a patty. Make sure your hands are lightly floured so the mixture does not stick to them.

6 Use the other half of the meat mixture to make the second rissole. Press the mixture together well to keep it from coming apart during cooking. Be sure to wash your hands after handling raw meat.

⓵7 Heat the oil in a frying pan. Cook the rissoles over medium heat for five minutes on each side. You can **broil** the rissoles rather than **fry** them if you like.

8 Garnish with tomato and onion slices. Serve hot with some sauerkraut or pickles.

FAST FOOD, GERMAN STYLE

The United States has made the hamburger a world-famous fast food. The Germans have created their own fast food, too. In Germany, hot dogs served with curry sauce are common snacks sold by vendors on the street.

Vienna-Style Escalopes

Escalope is the name for a thin, flat piece of meat. These breaded escalopes are very popular in Germany, where they are called Wiener Schnitzel (pronounced VEE-nuhr shnit-zul). Use pork or veal escalopes or pork tenderloin to make this dish.

What you need

6 slices of stale
  white bread
4 4-oz (115-g) pieces
  of pork or veal
2 tbsp lemon juice
1 egg
2 tbsp butter
2 tbsp vegetable oil
1 lemon

What you do

1 Place the bread onto a baking sheet.

2 **Preheat** the oven to 350°F (180°C). **Bake** the bread for ten minutes, or until it is crispy. Leave to cool.

3 Put the bread into a large bowl. Crush it to form bread crumbs. Pour the bread crumbs onto a plate.

4 Put a piece of meat between two pieces of plastic wrap. On a cutting board, pound the meat with a rolling pin or meat mallet to flatten it to a thickness of about ½ inch (1 cm). Remove the plastic wrap. Use kitchen shears to snip all around the edges of the meat. This will keep it from curling up as it cooks. Repeat this process for each piece of meat.

5 Put the meat and lemon juice into a resealable plastic bag. Shake well.

6 Lightly **beat** the egg and pour it onto a plate. Dip each piece of meat into the beaten egg, and then into the bread crumbs.

⊙ 7 Heat the butter and oil in a large frying pan. **Fry** the pieces of meat for two minutes on each side, or until the meat is cooked through. To see if it is cooked, make a small cut in the meat. It should not be pink inside.

8 Place on a plate and **garnish** with lemon slices. Serve the escalopes with boiled potatoes and green beans.

Potato Pancakes with Stewed Fruit

Potatoes are a common ingredient in German cooking. **Grated** pototoes are often made into **boiled** dumplings or fried into pancakes like these.

What you need

4 medium potatoes
½ an onion
1 egg
1 tbsp flour
4 tbsp vegetable oil

What you do

1 **Peel** the potatoes and grate them.

2 Peel the onion and grate it.

3 Lightly **beat** the egg. Mix together the grated potatoes, onion, flour, and egg. Add salt and pepper, and stir well.

4 Heat the oil in a nonstick frying pan. Add tablespoonfuls of the potato mixture to the frying pan with a little space in between them. (You may have to cook them in batches.) Flatten the potato cakes with a fork and **fry** for three to four minutes on each side, or until golden.

5 Serve with stewed apples (page 34) or stewed cranberries.

Stewed Cranberries

In Germany, cooked fruit is often served as a side dish alongside **savory** dishes. The fruit is cooked with only a little sugar so that it keeps its tangy taste.

What you do

1 Put 1 ½ cups (175 g) cranberries and 5 tablespoons of orange juice into a small saucepan. **Cover** and cook over low heat for ten minutes.

2 Stir from time to time to break up the cranberries. Add 4 tablespoons of sugar and stir until it has dissolved. Taste the fruit, adding a little more sugar if you wish.

3 Cool slightly and serve with potato pancakes.

Cabbage Rolls

Cabbage has been a **staple** food for Germans for hundreds of years. It is a vegetable that grows well in Germany, even in the north where it is cold. For this recipe choose a large cabbage and use the larger leaves, throwing away the tough outer leaves.

What you need

1 medium potato
1 small onion
4 oz (115 g) ground beef
4 oz (115 g) ground pork
2 slices bread
2 tsp dried parsley
¼ tsp nutmeg
1 egg, **beaten**
8 large cabbage leaves
4 bacon slices
1 tbsp vegetable oil
1 beef stock cube
salt and pepper

What you do

1 Scrub the potato. Cook it in **boiling** water with a pinch of salt for 20 minutes. **Drain** and leave it to cool.

2 **Peel** the onion and finely **chop** it. Put into a bowl with the meat.

3 Cut the bread into quarters and process it in a blender or food processor to make crumbs.

4 Add the bread crumbs to the meat mixture. Mix in the parsley, nutmeg, beaten egg, and a little salt and pepper.

5 **Peel** and **mash** the potato. Add it to the mixture.

6 Lay the cabbage leaves in a colander. Put the colander inside a heatproof bowl and place it in the sink.

7 **Cover** the cabbage leaves with boiling water. Leave for two minutes. Lift the colander out of the bowl to drain the cabbage leaves.

8 Spread one leaf out onto a cutting board. Spoon some meat filling onto the leaf and roll it up, tucking in the sides. Use a toothpick to hold the roll shut.

9 Repeat step 8 for each leaf.

①10 Chop the bacon. Heat the oil in a **Dutch oven** or large saucepan and **fry** the bacon for two minutes. Add the cabbage rolls and fry lightly all over.

11 Add enough hot water to cover the cabbage rolls. Crumble in the stock cube and bring it to a boil. Cover and **simmer** for 25 minutes.

12 Lift the cabbage rolls onto a plate and top with some of the cooking liquid. Serve hot with potatoes or potato dumplings (page 28).

27

Potato Dumplings

Potato dumplings are popular in Germany, where they are either made with cooked **mashed** potato, or with half mashed potato and half raw, **grated** potato as in this recipe. Use a mealy variety of potato, such as russets, for this dish.

What you need

8 medium potatoes
1 slice stale bread
3 tbsp oil
1 egg
½ cup (60 g) flour
1 ½ tsp fresh parsley, **chopped**

What you do

1 Peel the potatoes. Cook half of them whole for 20 minutes in **boiling** water with a pinch of salt. **Drain** them and leave them to cool.

(!) 2 To make croutons (small cubes of fried bread), cut the bread into small cubes. Heat the oil in a frying pan and gently **fry** the cubes until golden. Let them cool on a plate lined with paper towel.

3 **Mash** the cooked potatoes. Finely grate the raw potatoes. Mix the mashed and grated raw potatoes together. **Beat** in the egg, flour, and a pinch of salt.

4 Put 2 tablespoons of the potato mixture in your hand. Press a couple of croutons into the middle of the mixture.

5 Mold the potato mixture around the croutons to form a ball. Repeat this process until all of the potato mixture has been used.

6 Bring a pot of water to a boil. Add the dumplings and bring the water back to a boil. Lower the heat and **simmer** for ten to fifteen minutes, until the dumplings float to the top.

7 Place the dumplings on a dish and sprinkle with parsley. Serve hot with cooked meats and a little stewed fruit or sauerkraut.

Cooked Red Cabbage

During the winter months in Germany, people bake red cabbage to make this dish. It is usually eaten as part of an evening meal with potatoes and meat.

What you need

1 onion
1 red cabbage
2 red apples
2 tbsp vegetable oil
4 tbsp white
  wine vinegar
3 tbsp light
  brown sugar

What you do

1 **Peel** and finely **slice** the onion.

(!) **2** Throw away the outer leaves of the cabbage. With a sharp knife, cut the cabbage into quarters through the stalk. Cut out and throw away the stalk. Cut the leaves very finely to shred the cabbage.

3 **Preheat** the oven to 350°F (180°C). Peel the apples, cut out their cores, and **grate** the apples.

(!) **4** Heat the oil in a **Dutch oven. Fry** the sliced onion for two minutes. Add the cabbage and cook for four to five minutes stirring all the time.

5 Stir in the grated apple, 6 tablespoons of water, the vinegar, and the brown sugar. **Cover** tightly and put into the oven. Cook for 1 ½ to 2 hours.

6 Stir well and serve hot with potato dumplings (page 28) or cooked meats.

Red Cabbage and Bacon Salad

In Germany, salads of grated or sliced vegetables are often served before the main course with a little sugar and vinegar or lemon juice. This recipe makes enough for two people.

What you do

1 Finely slice enough red cabbage to make 2 full cups. Grate two carrots. Peel and slice one small onion.

2 Stir the vegetables together. Sprinkle with ½ teaspoon of caraway seeds, 1 teaspoon of sugar, and 2 teaspoons of vinegar.

3 Fry three pieces of bacon until crispy. When cool, finely chop the bacon. Stir the bacon pieces into the salad and serve.

Potato Salad

In Germany, people sprinkle their salads with vinegar, lemon juice, and a little sugar to give them a slightly sour taste. German potato salad has become a popular dish in the United States, and is sometimes served warm. For this salad, you can leave the skin on the potatoes if you want to.

What you need

2 lbs (900 g) small
  new potatoes
2 eggs
4 bacon slices (optional)
1 onion
2 gherkins
1 tbsp **capers** (optional)
1 beef stock cube
2 tbsp white wine vinegar
salt and pepper
lettuce leaves to **garnish**

What you do

1 Scrub the potatoes. Cook them whole in their skins in a pot of **boiling** water with a pinch of salt for 20 minutes. **Drain** and leave to cool.

2 While the potatoes are cooking, put the eggs in a saucepan. Cover them with water and bring to a boil. Turn down the heat and **simmer** for ten minutes.

3 Lift the eggs out with a spoon and place them in a bowl of cold water. Refill with fresh cold water until the eggs are cool.

4 **Fry** the bacon until it is crispy.

5 **Peel** and **chop** the onion.

6 Chop the gherkins, capers, and bacon. Peel the eggs and chop them.

7 **Slice** the potatoes. Stir the potatoes, onion, gherkins, capers, bacon, and chopped egg together.

8 Pinch off a small piece from the stock cube and dissolve it in 4 tablespoons of hot water. Mix it with the vinegar and pour it over the potatoes. Serve the salad with lettuce leaves arranged around it if you wish.

VARIATIONS

For a more meaty salad, add a sliced hot dog. For a **vegetarian** version, leave out the bacon and use a vegetable stock cube instead of a beef stock cube.

Stewed Apples

Germany has many orchards where apples and pears are grown, so fruit dishes and juices are popular throughout the country. Apples, especially, are used in both **savory** and sweet dishes. This dish goes well with potato pancakes (page 24). It is called *Apfelmus*.

What you need

2 lbs (900 g) apples
4 tbsp sugar

What you do

1 **Peel** the apples and **slice** them away from their cores into four or more pieces.

2 Put the apple pieces into a nonstick saucepan. **Cover** tightly and cook over low heat for five minutes, stirring now and then. (If you cook the apple too quickly, it will burn on the bottom of the pan.) Cook until the apple has softened.

3 Take the pan off the heat and stir in the sugar. Leave the mixture to cool. Add a little more sugar if you wish.

To cook in the microwave

Put the apple pieces in a microwave-safe bowl. Cover with a lid or plate and cook on high for two minutes. Stir and cook for 30 seconds more, or until the apple has softened. Stir in the sugar.

Storing apples

Whole apples don't freeze well, but stewed apples do. If you find yourself with a lot of apples in the autumn months, you can stew and freeze them to enjoy later.

Stew the apples as shown on page 34 and cool completely. Spoon them into plastic freezer bags and seal, leaving a little bit of space at the top of the bag for the mixture to expand as it freezes. When you want to use a bag of stewed apples, just **defrost** it overnight in the refrigerator.

Baked Cheesecake

Speisequark, or quark, is the most popular cheese in Germany. With a texture that is similar to cream cheese, it is often spread onto slices of bread and sprinkled with a little sugar.

What you need

1 package frozen pastry dough
flour for **dusting**
1 tsp lemon **zest**
1 lb (450 g) quark
6 tbsp honey
1 tbsp cornstarch
½ cup (60 g) raisins
2 eggs
1 tsp powdered sugar

What you do

1 **Preheat** the oven to 400°F (200°C). Put a baking sheet in to heat.

2 Dust a work surface and rolling pin with flour. Roll the rolling pin over the pastry dough. Turn the dough a little and roll it in another direction. Do this until it forms a circle about 12 inches (30 cm) wide.

3 Carefully lay the pastry into a tart pan with a removable bottom. Press it into the pan. Trim off any dough that is hanging over the edge by rolling the rolling pin over the top of the pan.

4 Chill the dough for ten minutes.

5 Place strips of foil around the inside edges of the dough to keep the sides straight during baking. Put it onto the hot baking sheet and bake for ten minutes.

6 In a bowl, mix together the quark, honey, cornstarch, raisins, and lemon zest.

7 To separate the eggs, crack one egg open carefully. Pass the yolk between the halves of the eggshell over a bowl until the white has dripped out into the bowl. Mix the yolk into the quark mixture. Do this with both eggs.

8 Using an electric mixer, beat the egg whites until they are firm. Use a metal spoon to **fold** the whites into the quark mixture.

9 Spoon the quark mixture into the baked pastry. Turn the oven down to 350°F (180°C) and bake the cheesecake for 35 to 45 minutes or until the filling becomes firm.

10 Let the cheesecake cool in the pan. Push the bottom of the pan up to lift out the baked cheesecake. Serve chilled and dusted with a little powdered sugar.

Black Forest Cake

This chocolate and cherry cake is a specialty of the Black Forest region of southwestern Germany. Morello cherries are slightly sour and taste best if they are cooked in a sugar syrup. You can buy them already prepared in jars or cans in the supermarket.

What you need

1 cup (210 g) sugar
1 cup (225 g) butter
4 eggs
3 tbsp cocoa
1 ¼ cup (150 g) self-rising flour
½ tsp baking powder
1 can or jar pitted morello cherries
2 ¼ cups (530 ml) whipping cream
3 oz (85 g) semisweet chocolate

What you do

1 **Preheat** the oven to 375°F (190°C). Cut out circles of parchment paper to fit the bottom of two 8-inch (20-cm) round cake pans. Grease the pans and line them with the parchment paper.

2 Using an electric mixer, **beat** the sugar and butter until the mixture is pale and creamy.

3 Beat the eggs and mix half of them into the butter mixture. Beat in the rest of the eggs, a little at a time.

4 Add the cocoa, flour, and baking powder to the mixture and **fold** in. Do this by cutting into the mixture with a spoon instead of stirring.

5 Spoon an equal amount of batter into each cake pan. Level the surface using the back of a spoon.

6 **Bake** for 20 minutes, or until the cake springs back when gently pressed in the center. Cool in the pans and then tip the cakes out onto a wire cooling rack.

7 **Drain** the liquid from the cherries. Using an electric mixer, beat the whipping cream until it is firm. Spread a quarter of it on top of one cake, and then scatter half of the cherries over it. Place the other cake on top.

8 Spread the top and sides of the cake with whipped cream, saving some for **piping.**

9 **Grate** the chocolate and press it onto the sides of the cake.

10 Pipe whipped cream around the top of the cake (see page 41) and put the rest of the cherries on top. Keep the cake chilled and serve the same day.

Raspberry Gelatin

Gelatin is a favorite food of both grown-ups and children in Germany. Fresh raspberries are best for this recipe, but if they are out of season you can use **defrosted** frozen raspberries instead. Strawberries and blackberries would work well in this recipe, too.

What you need

1 package raspberry-flavored gelatin
1 ½ cups (300 g) raspberries
⅔ cup (150 ml) whipping cream
sprigs of fresh mint to **garnish** (optional)

What you do

1 Open the package of gelatin and pour it into a heatproof glass bowl.

2 Very carefully pour the amount of **boiling** water indicated on the package instructions into the bowl. Stir until the gelatin powder has dissolved. Cool for ten minutes.

3 Divide half the raspberries between four small bowls and pour the gelatin over them. Put the bowls in the refrigerator to chill for about three hours.

4 Once the gelatin has cooled, arrange the rest of the raspberries equally on top of the four dishes.

5 Using an electric mixer or whisk, **beat** the whipping cream until it thickens.

6 **Pipe** cream on top of each dish of gelatin. If you prefer, you can just spoon the whipped cream on top instead.

7 Decorate each dish with a sprig of mint and serve chilled the same day.

PIPING WHIPPED CREAM

Put a piping tip into a piping bag. Spoon whipped cream into the piping bag.

Twist the top of the bag closed. Hold the twisted part of the bag between your thumb and first finger, with the palm of your hand resting on the bag. Hold the nozzle with your other hand. Squeeze the bag to squirt cream out of the nozzle.

Lebkuchen

Traditionally, these small, spicy cookies (pronounced LAYB-koo-ken) are eaten at Christmastime in Germany. **Monks** first baked lebkuchen over 700 years ago.

What you need

3 tbsp honey
2 tbsp sugar
1 tbsp vegetable oil
½ cup (50 g) dried apricots
2 tbsp candied citrus peel
1 tsp cocoa
¾ tsp cinnamon
¾ tsp cardamom
½ tsp cloves
1 cup (125 g) flour
1 ½ tsp baking powder
½ cup (55 g)
   ground hazelnuts
¼ cup (25 g)
   ground almonds
1 egg yolk

For the icing:
3 oz (85 g)
   semisweet chocolate
¾ cup (75 g)
   powdered sugar
assorted food coloring
sprinkles (optional)

What you do

1 Put the honey, sugar, and oil into a small nonstick saucepan. Heat on low and stir well. Let cool.

2 **Chop** the apricots and citrus peel very finely.

3 **Preheat** the oven to 325°F (170°C). In a large bowl, mix the cocoa, spices, flour, ground nuts, and baking powder together.

4 Add the honey mixture, the chopped fruits, and egg yolk to the dry mixture. Stir to form a stiff dough.

5 **Knead** the dough into a smooth ball. Roll it out until it is about ¼ inch (7 mm) thick.

6 Cut shapes out of the dough with small cookie cutters, or cut square or diamond shapes with a knife.

7 Place the cookies onto greased cookie sheets and **bake** for twelve to fifteen minutes. Cool them on a wire rack.

⊘ 8 Break the chocolate into a heatproof bowl and place it over a pan of **simmering** water. Stir from time to time until the chocolate has melted. Or, microwave the chocolate on high for one minute and stir until melted.

9 Using a fork, dip some of the cookies into the chocolate to coat them. Set them aside to harden.

10 Mix the powdered sugar with water, a teaspoonful at a time, to make a stiff icing. If you are using food coloring, divide the icing into three bowls and add a little coloring to each.

11 Spread or **pipe** icing (see page 41) onto some of the cookies and sprinkle them with sprinkles if desired. Cool and store in an airtight container.

More Books

Cookbooks

Hirst, Mike. *Germany*. New York: Raintree Steck-Vaughn, 1999.

Loewen, Nancy. *Food in Germany*. Vero Beach, Fla.: Rourke Publications, 1991.

Parnell, Helga. *Cooking the German Way*. Minneapolis, Minn.: Lerner Publications, 1989.

Books about Germany

Arnold, Helen. *Germany*. New York: Raintree Steck-Vaughn, 1995.

Boast, Clare. *Germany*. Chicago: Heinemann Library, 1998.

Comparing Weights and Measures

3 teaspoons=1 tablespoon	1 tablespoon=½ fluid ounce	1 teaspoon=5 milliliters
4 tablespoons=¼ cup	1 cup=8 fluid ounces	1 tablespoon=15 milliliters
5 ⅓ tablespoons= ⅓ cup	1 cup=½ pint	1 cup=240 milliliters
8 tablespoons=½ cup	2 cups=1 pint	1 quart=1 liter
10 ⅔ tablespoons=⅔ cup	4 cups=1 quart	1 ounce=28 grams
12 tablespoons=¾ cup	2 pints=1 quart	1 pound=454 grams
16 tablespoons=1 cup	4 quarts=1 gallon	

Healthy Eating

This diagram shows which foods you should eat to stay healthy. You should eat 6 to 11 servings a day of foods from the bottom of the pyramid. Eat 2 to 4 servings of fruits and 3 to 5 servings of vegetables a day. You should also eat 2 to 3 servings from the milk group and 2 to 3 servings from the meat group. Do not eat too many foods from the top of the pyramid.

German food includes plenty of bread, potatoes, and dumplings which belong to the bottom of the pyramid. Salads of raw **grated** vegetables are popular and healthy choices. Germans also enjoy many stewed fruits. Lunch meats and cheese, which are also popular, can be high in fat, so it's best not to eat too much of them.

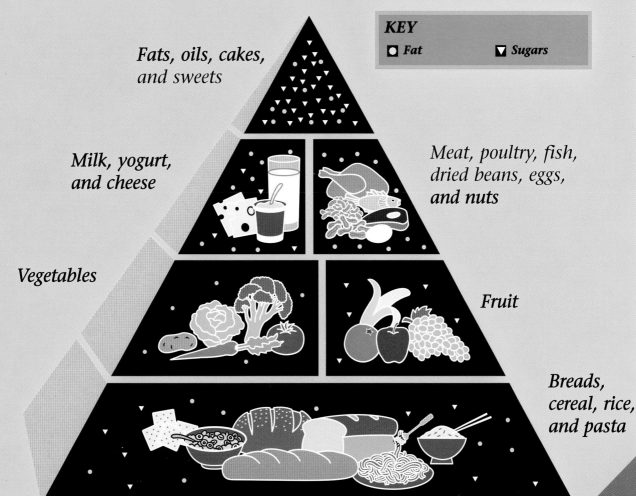

Fats, oils, cakes, and sweets

KEY

◻ Fat   ◻ Sugars

Milk, yogurt, and cheese

Meat, poultry, fish, dried beans, eggs, and nuts

Vegetables

Fruit

Breads, cereal, rice, and pasta

Glossary

bake to cook something in the oven

beat to mix something together strongly using a fork, spoon, or whisk

boil to heat liquid on the stove until it bubbles and steams strongly

broil to cook something under or over direct heat

caper seed of the nasturtium plant that has been pickled

chop to cut something into pieces with a knife

cover to put a lid on a pan or foil over a dish

defrost to bring something that has been frozen to room temperature

drain to remove liquid from a pan or can of food

dust to sprinkle something, such as powdered sugar, lightly over food

Dutch oven large iron cooking pot with a cover that can be used on the stove and in the oven

escalopes thin, flat slices of meat

ferment to undergo a chemical process that preserves food

fold to gently mix ingredients together with a metal spoon using cutting movements to keep air in the mixture

fry to cook something in oil or butter in a pan

garnish to decorate food for serving, for example, with fresh herbs or lemon wedges

grate to shred something by rubbing it back and forth over a utensil that has a rough surface

knead to mix ingredients into a smooth dough

lukewarm just barely warm

marinade sauce that food is left to soak in, so that the food absorbs the flavor of the sauce

mash to crush a food, such as potatoes or beans, until it is soft and smooth

monk member of a religious community of men who promise to obey a set of strict rules

peel to remove the outside of a fruit, vegetable, or hard-boiled egg

pipe to squeeze a topping onto food in decorative way using a special bag and tip

preheat to turn on the oven in advance, so that it is hot when you are ready to use it

savory not sweet

simmer to cook a liquid gently on the stove at just under a boil

slice to cut something into thin, flat pieces

staple main ingredient found in many dishes

vegetarian diet that usually does not include meat, poulty, or fish and that sometimes does not include eggs or dairy products. A person who follows such a diet is called a vegetarian.

whisk to beat air into ingredients by beating quickly with a utensil; the name of the wire utensil that is used for whisking together ingredients

zest outer layer of peel on a citrus fruit such as an orange or a lemon

Index